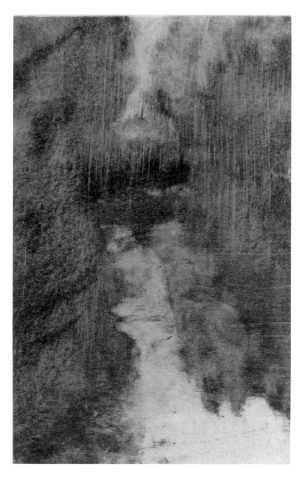

2
Small C & O Canal, 1997
monotype on *chine collé*
3½ x 2¼
Collection of the artist

2

3
Florentine Memories, 1976
oil on panel
4½ x 3⅝
Collection of the artist

INTIMATE IMPRESSIONS:

MONOTYPES AND PAINTINGS BY

Jack Boul

Essay by Eric Denker

THE CORCORAN GALLERY OF ART

WASHINGTON, D. C.

OCTOBER 28, 2000 — JANUARY 22, 2001

This catalogue was published on the occasion of the exhibition *Intimate Impressions: Monotypes and Paintings by Jack Boul.*
October 28, 2000 to January 22, 2001
The Corcoran Gallery of Art

Curator: Eric Denker, curator of prints and drawings
Exhibition Assistants: Emilie K. Johnson and Ken B. Ashton
Designer: Steve Kraft
Photographer: Lorene R. Emerson
Photography Assistant: David Applegate
Editor: Susan Badder

Printed by Alan Abrams Associates in association with Chromagraphics, Landover, Md.

The Corcoran Gallery of Art
500 Seventeenth Street NW
Washington, D. C. 20006-4804

This exhibition and catalogue were made possible in part by the support of the Evelyn Stefansson Nef Fund. The Nef Fund exhibition series highlights the work of mature artists whose life's work and ongoing achievement merit greater recognition and special attention in exhibition. Additional support for the catalogue has been generously provided by Kramerbooks and Afterwords, Inc., Washington D.C. Steve Kraft graciously contributed time and energy to the catalogue design.

Cover: *Museum Guard*, 1996, oil on gesso, 7¼" x 6", collection of Bette and Bob Reid.

Illustration 2: *Small C & O Canal*, 1997, monotype on *chine collé*, 3½" x 2¼", collection of the artist.

Illustration 3: *Florentine Memories*, 1976, oil on panel, 4½" x 3⅝", collection of the artist.

Back Cover: *Two-Sided Cow*, 1990, oil on board, 12½" x 14", collection of the artist

Library of Congress Cataloging-in-Publication Data

Boul, Jack, 1927-
  Intimate impressions : monotypes and paintings / by Jack Boul; essay by Eric Denker.
    p. cm.
  "October 28, 2000 to January 22, 2001, The Corcoran Gallery of Art."

  Includes index.
  ISBN 0-88675-061-X (alk. paper)
  1. Boul, Jack, 1927—Exhibitions. I. Denker, Eric. II. Corcoran Gallery of Art. III. Title.
  N6537.B643 A4 2001
  760'.092—dc21   00-011165

Acknowledgements

Foreword

I am deeply indebted to the many individuals whose dedication made possible both the catalogue and the exhibition of *Intimate Impressions: Monotypes and Paintings by Jack Boul.* From the Corcoran Gallery of Art staff I would like to thank Chief Curator Jackie Serwer and Vice-President of Finance and Administration Margaret Weiners. I would also like to thank Director of Corporate Relations Katy Ahmed, the Senior Director of Public Affairs and Marketing, Jan Rothschild, and her assistant Shannon Boland.

A special thanks to the Curator of Education, Susan Badder, for editing both catalogue and exhibition texts, and to our expert preparator Ken Ashton for his work on framing and installation. My thanks also to our registrars Victoria Fisher and Kimberly Davis for all of their help with the tracking of works, and to Exhibitions Coordinator Elizabeth Parr. The catalogue would not have been possible without the skilled assistance of Emilie K. Johnson, summer intern in the Prints and Drawings Department. Thanks also to Will Scott and Frances Feldman of the National Gallery of Art for their valuable editorial assistance.

We would also like to extend our appreciation to the many generous owners who lent treasured works to the exhibition, every loan request was graciously approved. A special note of gratitude is due to the Boul family for their encouragement throughout the development of the exhibition. Vivian Boul, the artist's wife, was particularly helpful, a model of spousal patience and support. David Boul, the artist's son, also provided important assistance in bringing the project to fruition. I would be remiss if I didn't reserve my most heartfelt thanks for the artist himself. Jack Boul has dedicated his life to the perfection of his art, working and teaching in the Washington area for the last half century. His career as an artist and teacher has enhanced the lives of the many students and art enthusiasts with whom he has come into contact. He is a perfectionist, diligent and hard working, and his gentle humor has helped make the project a thoroughly enjoyable endeavor.

I would like to extend my personal appreciation and gratitude to the *Nef Fund* for providing support for both the exhibition and the catalogue. I would also like to thank *Kramerbooks and Afterwords Café* for their valuable support of the catalogue.   E.D.

In the autumn of 1951, the Corcoran Gallery of Art held its *Sixth Annual Area Exhibition*, one of a series designed to promote the work of talented local artists. Two works by twenty-four-year old Jack Boul, recently relocated from Seattle, were included. Philip Evergood, Carl Zigrosser, and Chaim Gross were the distinguished jurors for the exhibition that introduced the young artist's work to the Washington public. In the following years Boul regularly exhibited in the Corcoran's area shows, as well as in group shows at the Smithsonian Institution, the Baltimore Museum of Art and many commercial galleries. In January of 1983, Jo Ann Lewis writing in *The Washington Post* about an exhibition at the Art Barn, commented that it was inexplicable that Boul had never had a one-man show in a local museum. A half-century after his initial showing, the Corcoran is pleased to address this oversight with *Intimate Impressions: Monotypes and Paintings by Jack Boul*, the artist's first one-man museum exhibition in Washington.

E.D.

INTIMATE IMPRESSIONS:
MONOTYPES AND PAINTINGS BY
JACK BOUL

Introduction

Jack Boul's art utilizes exceptional technical skill to convey a deeply poetic sensibility. His small-scale monotypes and paintings economically capture the timeless elements of the visible world. Landscape fascinates him, whether the rolling pastures of Maryland or the deserted beaches of North Carolina. Yet, the artist is as apt to be attracted to the gritty, cityscapes of Baltimore and Chicago as he is to the bucolic countryside. He depicts such familiar urban sights as water tanks and train yards with the same acuity he demonstrates when rendering the charm of a Parisian café or a Venetian canal. He is devoted to the beauty of the C & O Canal, and has a singular fondness for the shapes of cows. Boul's artistic interests extend from barnyards to barbershops, from wheelbarrows to watering cans. In both monotype and painting he returns to subjects repeatedly to explore the forms from different angles and in different formats. In each image, his spare, simple constructions convey the essential, characteristic elements of his motif.

Many of the artist's finest works center on the human figure and its myriad expressive possibilities. Occasionally he represents a model standing in the studio, while at other times he might select a solitary figure passing time on a park bench. Often Boul portrays groups of people, in a restaurant, in the loge of a theater, or simply seated around a table. Whether these encounters take place in public, or in a domestic or intimate space, they always speak to the artist's profound understanding of human relationships.

The intimate scale of the artist's works belies their monumental form and balance. Boul's subjects vary, but the content is always tempered by an appreciation of the compositional structure that informs the finest old master painting. While Boul prefers to work in the presence of his motif, or from drawings, he carefully avoids extraneous details; his monotypes and paintings seek the essence of their subjects, reducing the details of everyday surroundings to characteristic forms and gestures. As a teacher, Boul often reminded students of Delacroix's remark that the French painter only began to do something of value after he had forgotten enough small details to recall the really poetic and striking aspects of a theme. Boul's work transcends the actual appearance of his subject to obtain a more universal relevance. Although his art has remained steadfastly representational, he has always maintained that all art is essentially abstract, as much about relationships as about the ostensible subject matter. Boul is concerned with the relationships of light and dark areas, the contrast of sharp to soft edges, the balance between depth and surface, and the geometry of the composition. These issues are at the core of his artistic achievement, a body of work that reflects the artist's ongoing engagement with his environment, tempered by the search for more universal artistic truths.

Biography

Jack Boul was born in Brooklyn in 1927, and grew up in the South Bronx, the son of a Russian émigré father and a Romanian mother. He attended the American Artist's School in New York, before being drafted into the United States Army. In 1945-46 he served in an Engineers battalion as part of the U.S. occupational forces in and around Pisa, Italy. After the war, he moved to Seattle, Washington, where he studied on the GI Bill at the Cornish School of Art, graduating in 1951. Later that year he moved to the Washington, D.C. metropolitan area to continue his studies at American University. He exhibited in the Annual Area Exhibition at The Corcoran Gallery of Art in 1951, and again in 1954, 1956, and 1958. Boul also was represented in a number of group shows at the Baltimore Museum of Art in the 1950s. In 1956 he appeared in the *Sixty-Fourth Annual Exhibition of the Society of Washington Artists*, in a show juried and dominated by abstract expressionists. In an otherwise negative review of the exhibit, Florence Berryman of the Washington Star wrote, "The real puzzle picture in this show is Jack Boul's dainty naturalistic miniature *Olney Landscape*, somewhat primitive in effect, which seems as out of place here as a bon bon at a barbeque."[1]

In 1957 Jack Boul received his first solo showing, at the Franz Bader Gallery, attracting positive reviews that cited him as a promising young artist. In 1960 he had a one-man show at the Watkins Gallery of American University. In 1969 he was appointed to the art faculty at American University, and during his fifteen-year tenure he showed regularly at the Watkins Gallery. Boul had his first museum exhibition in 1974 at the Baltimore Museum of Art in a three-person exhibition that garnered several positive notices.

In 1984, after fifteen years at American University, Boul became one of the first faculty members of the new Washington Studio School. During ten years of teaching painting, drawing, and monotype, he had annual one-man shows in the Courtyard Gallery of the Studio School where he continues to show regularly. In 1986 Jack Boul was part of a two-person exhibition, with his friend the late Washington artist Peter DeAnna, at the Mint Museum in Charlotte, North Carolina. That exhibition was later shown at the University of Maryland in College Park. In addition he participated in numerous group exhibitions, most prominently the traveling show *Still Working: Under Known Artists of Age in America* to which he contributed eight oil paintings. The exhibition was shown locally at The Corcoran Gallery of Art. He retired from the Studio School in 1994 to devote his time to printmaking and painting.

Boul as Teacher: "There's Just One Little Thing..."
Jack Boul has taught in the Washington area since the 1950s. His students from Smithsonian classes, American University, and the Washington Studio School describe him as a soft-spoken but firm instructor, mixing words of praise for specific areas of a student work with insightful commentary on areas of weakness. He often starts tactfully by praising a particular passage, before beginning, "there's just one little thing...." He skillfully leavens his criticism with encouragement and with his dry, self-effacing sense of humor. Boul is recognized for his integrity and candor both as an artist and as a human being. He never shrinks from offering honest criticism, whether of a student's work or of the paintings of contemporaries, or even acknowledged old masters. He laces his instruction with examples of great artists of the past, invoking Rembrandt, Velasquez, Corot, Sargent, Whistler, Vuillard, and Eakins with great affection.

Boul's teaching philosophy always begins with the larger elements of composition. He has often paraphrased the French nineteenth-century painter Camille Corot, instructing students not to be in a hurry to get to details, but first and foremost to be interested in the masses and larger patterns of the picture. Sometimes Boul would project slides of famous works deliberately out of focus so the students would not recognize the image but see the larger areas of light and dark. He stresses the inner geometry of the picture, the shapes and divisions within the compositional structure, and the relationship of the component parts of a painting. Despite emphasizing the importance of structure, Boul always has denied the possibility of a formula that could be employed as a short cut to composition. Each artistic decision is formulated on the demands of the particular arrangement and the sensibility of the artist. Boul's teaching principles reveal his approach to the underlying structure of his monotypes and paintings.

Monotypes: Technique and Composition
Jack Boul was involved in printmaking throughout the early part of his career, but he only began to experiment with monotype in the early 1970s. In the monotype process, an artist creates an image by painting with viscous ink on the surface of a blank plate. The ink on the plate can be worked and reworked until the artist is satisfied with the design, and then printed by hand or with an intaglio press. The image is called a monotype, since only one vivid impression can be made from the design on the plate. Monotype is the most direct and painterly of all print processes, paralleling the technique and resulting appearance of the oil medium. The fluid surface can be manipulated for a variety of different effects, whether a bright sunlit landscape or dark interior spaces. Though the monotype process is at odds with the traditional function of printmaking, which is to make multiple originals, it has become one of the most popular forms of printing today.

The Genoese artist Giovanni Benedetto Castiglione pioneered the use of monotype in the mid-seventeenth century, but only in the late nineteenth century was the process widely accepted. Degas was the greatest proponent of monotype, learning the process from Comte Ludovic-Napoleon Lepic, an obscure printmaker of the era. The French artists Pissarro, Gauguin, and Toulouse-Lautrec all experimented with the medium, as did Picasso, but Americans have had the greatest interest in the expressive potential of monotype. Maurice Prendergast, John Sloan, and Robert Henri utilized monotype in the early years of this century, while Milton Avery, Mark Tobey, Richard Diebenkorn, and Wayne Thiebaud have exploited the potential of the medium in contemporary art.

Jack Boul has always maintained that monotype is the easiest technique to learn, simply involving painting or drawing on a blank surface, and then printing. Though the technique is easily acquired, mastery of the process requires discipline and perseverance. In many cases Boul executes an image quickly, retaining a sense of the immediacy of creation. The artist prints the monotype on the bed of a small proof press, placing a sheet of moistened paper over the plate. He uses a layer of felt blankets over the paper to apply an even amount of pressure. Boul finds the moment of printing is exhilarating and suspenseful, since in monotype the transfer of the surface ink from the plate to the paper is highly unpredictable. The result may be a revelation or a disappointment. At times the artist gains the desired result on the first pass through the press, at other times he reworks the image remaining on the plate with additional ink and brushwork. Boul may be pleased with one part of a print, but feel that other sections are less successful. He sometimes keeps an impression because there is some aspect of it that interests him, but he is a perfectionist who only regards approximately one out of twenty images as a completed work.

In his monotypes, Boul employs an array of sophisticated techniques to create subtlety in his designs. By diluting the black ink with turpentine, the artist can produce an infinite range of grays; the gradation of values in a monotype often suggests color. Although occasionally Boul has produced color prints, he prefers black etching ink for his monotypes. The artist can affect the thickness of the ink and the painterly qualities of the edges and lines by varying the pressure of the press and the number of felt blankets that are used in printing. Sometimes Boul begins a design on an un-inked blank plate, at other times he covers the surface with ink and creates an image by wiping white areas out from the dark background. He may use his fingers, or large brushes, or cotton swabs to create an image, depending on whether a particular subject requires crisp outlines or soft contours.

Boul approaches monotype with the same principles as he does painting. No distinction exists in the artist's mind between the acts of painting and printmaking. Many times Boul treats the same subject in both media, creating images in color and in black and white. The inspiration for an oil may precede a monotype or vice-versa, with no set pattern. A monotype may be a mirror image of a painting, or it may have a parallel orientation. Throughout he remains interested in the larger compositional relationships, areas of dark and light, of form and of space, and of the division of the surface into its basic geometry. The artist has an ongoing interest in the relationship of masses and voids in his compositions. He often has made reference to the ideas of the Chinese philosopher Lao Tzu, who said that while the material contains utility, the immaterial contains essence.

The Subjects of the Artist
Boul has a strong predilection for landscape. His pictures capture a broad range of motifs varied by specific seasonal conditions. We see the C & O Canal in spring or in autumn, in brilliant sunlight or under cool, gray, overcast skies (plate 10). The artist subtly describes a steamy summer afternoon in the rolling hills and valleys of Frederick County, or the almost imperceptible morning haze that hangs over a Tuscan countryside.

Boul repeatedly returns to favorite subjects, often over a long period of time, to explore the expressive possibilities of a theme. The artist never intended these works to be exhibited serially, but seeing a group of images inspired by the same motif reveals the variety of solutions offered by different formats and approaches. Boul's many images of the C & O Canal, for example, were produced over a thirty-year period, and show immense variation in size, shape,

color, cropping, and focus (plates 2, 4, 5, 6, 8, 9, 10, and 11). While stressing the essentially abstract nature of painting, Boul has remained steadfastly representational in his approach to the subjects of his monotypes and paintings. On occasion, however, his work pushes the limits of representation, as in the spare *Abstract Landscape* (plate 12) for example.

His paintings have often been compared to the work of Camille Corot, or the Barbizon School, artists he esteems, but the resemblance is more in the subject matter than in the handling. Boul's application of paint and tonal harmonies are more closely related to the approach of Silvestro Lega, Giuseppe Abbati, and Giovanni Fattori, members of the Italian Macchiaioli group that the artist has long admired. Boul is an avid student of art history, but though his work resonates with the knowledge of the past, his images remain resolutely contemporary, transcending any connections to the old masters. Landscapes such as *Hoeing* (plate 29), *Queen Anne's Lace* (plate 45), and *A Corner in the Country* (plate 27) are distinctly American images of our time.

While Boul acknowledges the inspiration of a particular subject, he resists the identification of his pictures with specific people and places. He prefers generic rather than informative titles. Figures are rarely named, landscapes and cities are unidentified. He prefers that his work evoke the universal rather than define the particular. Boul is in agreement with an artist he admires, James McNeill Whistler, who said that nature rarely produces the harmony worthy of a great picture, but that the artist must pick and choose to produce the arrangement necessary for a great work of art.

A number of Boul's most innovative landscapes are the result of a radical simplification of the pictorial means. The monotypes *Canal Path* (plate 6) and *Abstract Landscape* (plate 12) use a few suggestive brush strokes to convey the artist's perception of nature. Boul has always esteemed the economy of Rembrandt's landscape drawings, and his work reflects an affinity for the Dutch master's spare vocabulary. Similarly, Boul's diminutive images of beaches reduce the composition to a few essential horizontal bands only interrupted by clouds above, or by rocks in the surf below (plate 34). These minimalist compositions are strongly reminiscent of the economy of Whistler's seascape sketches.

Jack Boul grew up in the 1930s in the inner city, and has always retained an affection for urban forms. He approaches cityscape seeking a solid geometric underpinning for the formal elements of his design. Views across rooftops provide Boul with a series of forms and shapes that appeal to his artistic sensibility (plate 139). He renders unromantic urban motifs such as railway yards (plate 38), trestles, and water tanks (plate 18) with the sympathetic eye of the city dweller. *Chicago Underpass* (plate 20) is a characteristic example, exploiting the basic geometry of the architecture as the foundation of the pictorial contrast of mass and space. The artist emphasizes the essential flatness of the design by allowing the grain and warm tone of the under panel to subtly merge into the foreground.

The balance between the surface patterns and the creation of depth, and the integration of open spaces and strong architectural elements are a hallmark of some of Boul's finest works. In *Venetian Alley* (plate 25), the artist balances the sun-lit bricks and stucco of the wall with the shadows and depth of the passageway. In the related monotype, *Sottoportico* (plate 21) the pictorial elements are even more radically simplified, the entire right side of the composition barely suggested by a light gray wash of ink.

Similarly, Boul's interiors are arrangements of light and dark masses dictated by the geometry of windows, mirrors, frames, and furniture. In the early *Hyattsville Studio* (plate 60) the artist balances the rectangles of the windows and the reflections on the floor with the geometry of the desk and easel. Boul used a similar tack in the evocative monotype *Venetian Light* (plate 32) with its strong morning sun penetrating the shadows of the Gothic palace through the Moorish fifteenth-century windows. The glare of light is contrasted to the firm structure of the windows and walls. *Museum Guard* (cover), a tonal masterpiece, is also a meditation on the use of framing devices. The painting contains a marvelous play of rectangular shapes, the form of the central door mimicking the shape of the canvas, and playing off against the walls, the wainscoting, the picture frames, and the truncated doorjamb in the background. The lines of the pediment and the gently curved profile of the seated guard discretely soften the severe angularity of the design. Boul tackles a more complex space in *Reflections, Café Interior* (plate 78) where the mirrors reflect a complicated set of spaces. The spatial arrangements of restaurants and cafés fascinate the artist, and he has returned to the theme throughout his career. Boul's many images of Haussner's Restaurant in Baltimore (plates 74, 76, 79, and 97) are explorations of the linear structure of the wall decoration used as a foil for the oval shapes of tables and for the couples seated in the foreground. Small human figures inhabit many of the interiors, an integral element in the overall design. In *Reading* (plate 84) the seated woman in the rocking chair is an essential part of

the design, absorbed into the tonal harmony in a fashion evocative of the flat, decorative effects in a painting by Vuillard. The artist always has been attracted to people engaged in everyday public and personal activities. *The Entertainer* (plate 93) captures a performance on the stage of an old music hall. *The Barbershop* (plate 141) is a depiction of familiar, quotidian business. Boul's images also can be intimate, charged with emotional overtones, as in *The Proposition* (plate 52), or *The Edge of the Bed* (plate 54). The soft focus and suggestive quality of the monotype process is especially well suited for provocative imagery.

Many of Boul's works focus on the figure as a major compositional element. Sometimes he depicts simply a head, or a bust length figure, isolated from the surrounding environment. Many of his figures are lost in thought, captured in poses characteristic of age or fatigue (plate 65). Boul's figures inhabit museums (plate 69), quiet cafés (plate 81), or elaborately decorated, domestic interiors (plate 96). Sometimes they sew, weave, or garden (plate 94), but they rarely move. *Tango* (plate 134) and the related sculpture (plate 127) are rarities in Boul's *oeuvre* as descriptive of arrested motion.

The human figure also is prominent in one of the most unusual of all of Boul's works, the *Holocaust Series* (plates 118-126). The artist served in the European theatre just after the war. He was profoundly affected by the unfolding stories of the Holocaust. He has written:

In 1946 I was a sergeant with the U.S. Army Engineers Corps stationed at a prisoner of war camp outside Pisa, Italy. I remember showing German prisoners of war pictures of the liberated concentration camps. They refused to believe the pictures. "You have your propaganda and we have ours."

In 1986, I saw the documentary *Shoah* and was very moved. It showed the cattle cars that transported people to the concentration camps, the furnaces where people were cremated, and the fields where the ashes were scattered. It never showed the victims. I remembered the photographs I had seen in Italy forty years earlier, and decided to look for other photos of the camps.

In the United States Archives I found hundreds of photographs from many different concentration camps. I looked at the photos for days, and made drawings. In my studio, I made these monotypes from the drawings. I wanted to make something that would help to keep that memory alive.[2]

Boul's stark images of the Holocaust Series are his attempt to convey the horror of the concentration camps, and to memorialize this dark moment of recent history. The artist portrays emaciated corpses, individually or heaped one upon another. Barely perceptible bodies are

FIGURE 1. *Wheelbarrow*, 1987, Monotype, 5 x 6⅞,
Ronald Costell and Marsha Swiss

strewn in awkward positions, skulls with jaws agape scream out in horror.

While the subject of the series is the nightmare of the Holocaust, the more universal content examines man's capacity for inhumanity towards other men. As with Callot's *Miseries and Misfortunes of War* from 1633, and Goya's *Disasters of War* from 1810-14, Boul's moving images both portray and transcend the specific circumstances to become a moving commentary on human suffering.

Cows are a great favorite of the artist, who regularly drives out to the countryside in search of animals to draw. Boul is attracted to their shapes and silhouettes, individually (plate 102) as well as in groups (plate 115), standing (plate 114) and lying down (plate 145). In landscapes, he is interested in the way cows help to tie a composition together, either as a solid mass or to establish depth. He depicts them in infinite combinations, often overlapping and blending individual creatures together to make interesting and unusual forms (plate 112). He has often said to students, "cows do a lot more than stand out there and just eat and moo." Cows have become a signature subject with Boul, who depicts them standing in pastures (plate 116) and in paddocks (plate 40), involved in all types of characteristic bovine behavior—scratching, eating, sleeping, and drinking (plates 111 and 152).

Boul also is attracted to the shapes of birds. He depicts them singly (plate 137) and in clusters on feeders (plate 107). He renders them flocked together on electrical wires, becoming the aviary equivalent of a musical score (plate 91). The purity and directness of these depictions are reminiscent of Wallace Stevens' poem, *Thirteen Ways of Looking at a Blackbird*. Boul also portrays individual dead birds (plates 92, 105 and 106), part of a long tradition that extends from Baroque game pieces to Albert Pinkham Ryder's small oil painting at The Phillips Collection. These small yet poignant images refer inevitably to a meditation on death. Similarly, Boul's image of *Kosher Chickens* (plate 104) can be read as both a reference to a familiar motif from the artist's past, and as symbolic of mortality.

The simple shape and sleek lines of a wheelbarrow, a common garden implement, provide Boul with a motif of great purity (figure 1). Writing in *The Washington Post* in 1988, Paul Richard described his reaction to this image. "'Wheelbarrow' by Jack Boul lingers in the memory like the fragment of a melody. Its scale is domestic (it's not much bigger than a postcard). Its theme is unheroic. That lovely little monotype—it's half painting and half print—could hardly be more modest, yet I've thought of it all day. Its colors are subdued. They are only blacks and grays, and yet they manage to imply the quiet buzzing of midsummer, the glare of midday sunshine, the warm weight of the air and the deep green of the grass."[3]

The simplicity of the image results from Boul's exacting distillation of the essential nature of the wheelbarrow, its volume and its shape. Nothing is inherently picturesque in this homely vehicle, yet Boul endows it with a timelessness and monumentality beyond the scope of its humble function. His paintings and monotypes reveal the underlying structure of the world around us. The wheelbarrow is an ideal metaphor for Jack Boul's achievement. He creates intimate works of balance and harmony, images of surpassing beauty drawn from the fabric of everyday life. Throughout his career as an painter and a teacher, Boul has been a model of perseverance and artistic integrity, persistently seeking the perfection of his art.

---

[1] Florence S. Berryman, "Washington Artists Show Disappointing," *The Washington Star*, undated clipping (October, 1956), *Boul Family Scrapbook*, volume I.
[2] Written statement from the artist to the author.
[3] Paul Richard, "Jack Boul's Quiet Power," *The Washington Post*, April 16, 1988, page C2.

All catalogue measurements are presented in inches, height preceding width.

4
Moonlight, N.D.
oil on museum board
7¾ x 5½
Nina Boul Rasch and
Gustav A. Rasch III

5
Canal Reflections, 1976
monotype
11¼ x 8¼
Dick Youniss

6
Canal Path, 1976
monotype
6 x 6¾
Collection of
Gloria Monteiro Rall

7
Green and Black #2, 1972
oil on canvas
3 x 5¼
Collection of the artist

8
C & O Canal, Autumn,
1985
oil on museum board
7¾ x 10½
Collection of
David H. Boul

9
C & O Canal, 1987
monotype
11¾ x 15½
Collection of the artist

10
C & O Canal, 1972
oil on canvas
12 x 15
Collection of the artist

11
C & O Canal, 1972
oil on canvas
12 x 15
Collection of the artist

12
Abstract Landscape, 2000
monotype
5 x 7
Collection of the artist

13
Rocks and Breakers, 1997
oil on museum board
4¼ x 7
Collection of the artist

14
Waves, 1992
oil on panel
4¾ x 8¾
Collection of the artist

15
Small Landscape, 1996
oil on museum board
3¾ x 5⅞
Collection of the artist

16
Clouds and Sand, 1990
oil on canvas
4⅝ x 6⅞
Lee and Sue Newman

17
French Archway, 1992
oil on canvas
13¼ x 10
Collection of the artist

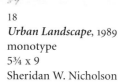

18
Urban Landscape, 1989
monotype
5¾ x 9
Sheridan W. Nicholson

19
Railroad Trestle, 1989
oil on panel
4½ x 7
Kyropoulos/Tenney
Collection

20
Chicago Underpass, 1990
oil on panel
8 x 9½
Collection of the artist

21
Sottoportico, 1995
monotype
4½ x 7⅞
Private Collection

22
Barn Light, 1999
oil on panel
6½ x 11
John M. Shank and
Joseph O. Matthews

23
Overpass, 1990
oil on canvas
9 x 16
Collection of Bette
and Bob Reid

24
Barn Light, 1998
monotype
6 x 9
Private Collection

25
Venetian Alley, 1996
oil on canvas
8 x 12
Collection of Dr. and
Mrs. Robert Martin

26

26
Horizontal Seascape, 1991
oil on museum board
4¾ x 8½
Collection of the artist

27
A Corner in the Country, 1995
oil on museum board
6⅜ x 9
Robert and Mary Heiderer

28
**Hazy Day in
Frederick,** 1994
oil on panel
4½ x 7
Kyropoulos/Tenney
Collection

29
Hoeing, 1971
oil on canvas
9 x 12
Ann M. Faegre

30
View from Whistler's Window, 1995
monotype
4⅛ x 8
Private Collection

31
Elevators, 1992
monotype
3⅛ x 7
Collection of the artist

32
Venetian Light, 1996
monotype
8 x 11
Gift of the Friends of
The Corcoran Gallery of Art

33
Entrance to the El, 1988
oil on canvas
7¼ x 5¼
Kyropoulos/Tenney
Collection

34
Beach Scene, 1997
oil on museum board
5¾ x 9¾
Kyropoulos/Tenney
Collection

35
Farm Scene, 1987
oil on canvas
6 x 8⅜
Sheridan W. Nicholson

36
Industrial Shapes, 1987
monotype
5¼ x 6⅞
Collection of the artist

37
Viaduct, 1995
monotype
4½ x 7½
Ronald Costell and
Marsha Swiss

38
Railroad Yard, 1989
monotype
5½ x 9
Collection of the artist

39
Baltimore Corner, 1985
monotype
4 x 6
Collection of
David H. Boul

40
Cows Before a Barn,
1993
oil on panel
6⅜ x 9
Megan Greene

41
Summer Light, Provence, 1997
monotype
5 x 7
Private Collection

42
Queen Anne's Lace,
1997
oil on museum board
5¾ x 8
Collection of the artist

43
Wooden Gate, 1993
oil on panel
5¾ x 7½
Collection of the artist

44
Landscape, 1991
oil on panel
5 x 7⅞
Dr. Robert Gillman

45
Queen Anne's Lace, 1996
monotype
5 x 7
Gift of the Friends of
The Corcoran Gallery
of Art

46
The Church, 1990
monotype
6¼ x 4
Juliana Weihe

47
Cathedral Interior, 1995
monotype
7⅞ x 5¾
Private Collection

48
Long Shadows, 1996
oil on museum board
7 x 10
Collection of
Carla D'Arista

49
Long Shadow, 1996
monotype
5¾ x 7⅞
Collection of
Thomas L. O'Briant, Jr.

50
Clouds, 1984
oil on canvas
7½ x 9½
Collection of
the artist

51
Pergola, 1995
oil on panel
6¼ x 10
Collection of the artist

52
The Proposition, 1989
monotype
6⅝ x 4
Collection of Joey
and
Lynne Kossow

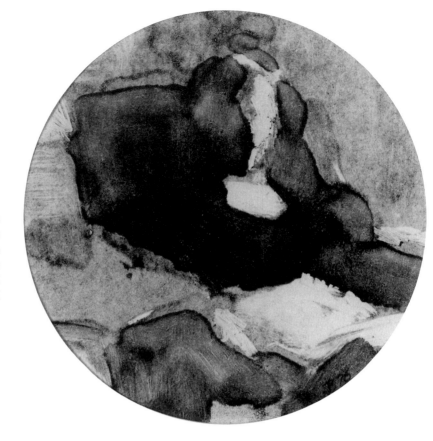

53
Seated Figure, 1976
monotype
3½ diameter
Nina Boul Rasch and
Gustav A. Rasch III

54
Edge of the Bed, 1993
monotype
5⅛ x 6⅞
Collection of
Elizabeth Naden

58
Self-Portrait, 1985
oil on canvas
11¾ x 8¾
Collection of the artist

59
The Meal, 1991
monotype
4 x 5¾
Private Collection

60
Hyattsville Studio, 1965
oil on masonite
9⅞ x 14
Collection of
Ethel Weichbrod

48

61
Rug Menders, 1985
monotype
4 x 6
Collection of
Starr Kopper

62
Two Figures in a Café, 1990
oil on panel
6 x 7⅞
Kyropoulos/Tenney
Collection

63   49
Large Rug Menders, 1985
monotype
15½ x 11¾
Collection of the artist

64
Black Stockings, 1989
monotype
6½ x 4
Margaret and
Terry Lenzner

65
Man on a Bench, 1988
monotype
6 x 4
Juliana Weihe

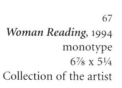

66
Blacksmith, 1984
monotype
7 x 5¼
Private Collection

67
Woman Reading, 1994
monotype
6⅞ x 5¼
Collection of the artist

68
Reading, 1993
monotype
5 x 6⅞
Robert and
Mary Heiderer

69
Museum Guard, 1993
monotype
7 x 5¼
Collection of
David H. Boul

70
Man Reading, 1984
oil on canvas
7¾ x 5¾
Collection of the artist

53

71
Two Figures, 1987
monotype
7⅞ x 9⅞
Collection of the artist

72
The Fur Coat, 1983
monotype
6¾ x 5¼
On loan from Ursula
and Frank Ferro

73
The Loge, 1986
monotype
7 x 8⅝
Collection of
David H. Boul

74
Haussner's II, 1989
monotype
4 x 6
Collection of Joey
and Lynne Kossow

75
Paris Café, 1992
oil on canvas
8 x 10
Collection of Bette
and Bob Reid

76
Haussner's, 1989
monotype
5 x 7
Private Collection

77
Woman at a Table, 1990
monotype
5½ x 4⅞
Robert and Mary Heiderer

78
*Reflections, Café
Interior*, 1998
oil on canvas
14 x 20
Collection of the artist

58

79
Haussner's, 1989
monotype
7 x 5
Anonymous gift in honor
of Jack Cowart
The Corcoran Gallery of Art

80
The Conversation, 1993
monotype
6 x 5
Collection of the artist

81
Parisian Café, 1993
Oil on museum board
6⅛ x 8⅝
Collection of Jack Barrett
and Lauren Sanders

82
Venetian Palace, 1997
oil on museum
board
6 x 4
Kyropoulos/Tenney
Collection

83
Theatre Box, 1978
monotype
4 x 5⅞
Private Collection

85
Blue Interior, 1974
oil on canvas
14¼ x 5⅝
Nina Boul Rasch and
Gustav A. Rasch III

84
Reading, n.d.
oil on museum board
9 x 5⅜
Ronald Costell and
Marsha Swiss

62

86
Cows in a Wood, 1981
oil on panel
4 x 7⅞
Collection of the artist

87
Three Men on a Bench, n.d.
oil on canvas
6 x 8
Collection of the artist

88
Small Head, 1982
drypoint
2⅜ x 1⅝
Collection of the artist

89
Pelican, 1989
monotype
5⅞ x 8⅞
Julian Brunner

64

90
Standing Nude, n.d.
oil on panel
6⅞ x 4½
Collection of the artist

91
Nineteen Birds, 1992
monotype
5 x 7
Collection of the artist

92
Carolina Wren, 1995
oil on museum board
5 x 7½
Collection of the artist

93
The Entertainer, 1995
monotype
5½ x 4⅞
Collection of Dr. and
Mrs. Robert Martin

94
Gardening, 1991
monotype
6 x 8⅞
Collection of the artist

95
Chicago Parlor, 1998
oil on canvas
11 x 16
Collection of
David H. Boul

96
French Interior, 1998
oil on board
9½ x 7⅛
Collection of the artist

97
Haussner's III, 1988
monotype
6¼ x 3⅞
Private Collection

98
Cows in a Gully, 1991
monotype
8 x 11
Private Collection

99
Repairing Rugs, 1985
oil on canvas
7 x 11
Collection of the artist

100
Lonely Café, 1996
monotype
6 x 8¾
Collection of John and
Mimi Herbert

101
Vase of Flowers, 1983
monotype
9⅞ x 8
The Washington Post
Company

102
Holstein, 1990
oil on canvas
8 x 12
Collection of the artist

103
Line of Cows, 1976
monotype
4¾ x 11½
Estate of Robert D'Arista

72

104
Kosher Chickens, 1988
monotype
4¾ x 3⅞
Private Collection

105
Dead Bird, 1985
monotype
2¾ x 4
Collection of Bette
and Bob Reid

106
Dead Bird, 1985
monotype
2¾ x 4
Ronald Costell and
Marsha Swiss

107
Birds on a Feeder, 1989
monotype
6⅞ x 3¾
Collection of the artist

108
Wheelbarrow, 1990
monotype
3⅞ x 6¼
Collection of Bette
and Bob Reid

109
Wheelbarrow, 1989
monotype
4 x 6
Sheridan W. Nicholson

110
Wheelbarrow, 1990
monotype
10⅞ x 7⅜
Gift of the Friends of
The Corcoran Gallery
of Art

111
Cows in a Barn, 1973
encaustic on masonite
3⅜ x 5½
Collection of the artist

112
Ten Cows, 1991
oil on canvas
5 x 12½
Kyropoulos/Tenney
Collection

113
Cow Before a Barn, 1997
monotype
5 x 7
Collection of the artist

114
Cows in the Shade, 1991
oil on panel
5 x 8
Kyropoulos/Tenney
Collection

115
Line of Cows, 1988
monotype
5 x 11
Collection of
Starr Kopper

116
Cows, n.d.
oil on canvas
5 x 13½
Collection of
the artist

117
Cow in a Barn, 1993
monotype
5 x 7
On loan from
Ursula and Frank Ferro

120
Holocaust Series (g), 1986
monotype
4¾ x 4
Collection of the artist

121
Holocaust Series (h), 1986
monotype
7¾ x 11
Collection of the artist

122
Holocaust Series (i), 1986
monotype
5 x 6⅞
Collection of the artist

123
Holocaust Series (c), 1986
monotype
11 x 7⅞
Collection of the artist

124
Holocaust Series (d), 1986
monotype
4 x 2¾
Collection of the artist

125
Holocaust Series (e), 1986
monotype
4¾ x 4
Collection of the artist

126
Holocaust Series (f),
1986
monotype
6 x 8¾
Collection of the artist

127
Tango, 1999
bronze
7¼ x 4 x 2½
Collection of
the artist

128
Head, 1999
bronze
2½ x 2 x 1½
Collection of
the artist

129
Sitting Cow, 1973
wax over fired clay
2¾ x 7 x 5
Collection of the artist

130
Cow's Head, 1974
epoxy over wax
3½ x 3¾ x 4
Collection of
the artist

131
Bird, 1999
bronze
3½ x 6¼ x 2¼
Collection of
the artist

132
Cow Scratching, 1999
bronze
3½ x 4 x 2
Collection of the artist

133
Seated Figure, 1980
epoxy over wax
4 x 2¼ x 3
Collection of
the artist

134
Tango, 1998
monotype
6½ x 4
Collection of the artist

135
Cows in a Grove, 1985
monotype
8 x 9¾
Nina Boul Rasch and
Gustav A. Rasch III

136
Seated Figure, 1980
epoxy over wax, wood base
4½ x 3 x 3¾
Collection of the artist

137
Bird, 1994
encaustic on masonite
5¼ x 4½
Collection of the artist

138
Trees, 1985
monotype
11½ x 15⅞
Collection of the artist

139
Rooftops, 1988
oil on canvas
6⅜ x 12
Collection of the artist

140
Bird on a Perch, 1989
monotype
6⅞ x 3¾
Joyce Jewell and
Wilfred Brunner

94

141
Barbershop, 1978
oil on canvas
9 x 12
Estate of
Robert D'Arista

142
Three Figures, 1982
oil on panel
4 x 6½
Collection of
the artist

143
Tuscany, 1976
monotype
8¼ x 11
Dick Youniss

144
Studio Interior,
1985
monotype
9⅞ x 7⅞
Collection of
the artist

145
Milking Stall, 1986
oil on canvas
4½ x 7⅛
Collection of
the artist

146
Quartet, 2000
oil on canvas
12 x 14
Collection of Mira and
Yankl Stillman

147
Wheelbarrow, 1988
oil on panel
7⅞ x 6
Dr. Robert Gillman

148
Seated Figure, 1976
monotype
3⅞ x 3¼
Ken and Pat Moss

150
C & O Canal, 1995
oil on gesso
5½ x 8
Mr. and Mrs. Ben
Summerford

149
Couple Dancing, 1997
monotype
5⅞ x 4
Private Collection

151
Landscape, 1963
etching, 2/15
5 x 5⅞
Collection of Lee Heys

152
Feeding, 1985
monotype
5⅛ x 6⅞
Collection of Maureen
and Tom O'Connor